THE PRACTICE OF

Humility

60 COUNSELS ON DEEPING THIS VIRTUE

Pope Leo Xiii

FOREWORD BY BISHOP ATHANASIUS SCHNEIDER

SENSUS FIDELIUM PRESS

Gastonia, North Carolina

Paperback: 978-1-962639-02-6
E-book: 978-1-962639-03-3
Cover image:
Page layout design by Faith & Family Publications.

For more information, please visit *sensusfideliumpress.com*

Printed in the United States of America

Contents

Discite a Me quia mitis sum et humilis corde.
Learn of Me, because I am meek and humble of heart.
—Matthew 11:29

Humilibus dat gratiam.
To the humble He giveth grace.
—1 Peter 5.5

Foreword

The greatest example of humility is our Lord Jesus Christ himself. The true foundation of humility is, therefore, found in the example of God himself, made man. "Humility is so important for man, that the divine majesty wanted to recommend it also with his example. The proud man would have been lost forever if God had not come looking for him by humbling himself. In fact, the Son of man came to seek and to save what was lost (Luke 19:10). The man was lost for having followed the pride of the tempter; therefore, now that he has been found, let him follow the humility of the Redeemer" (St. Augustine, *In Ioan.* tr. 55, 7) The spiritual building of the Christian soul must, therefore, have a profound foundation of humility, which is established in the truth of the Incarnation of God.

"There are more saints in heaven who have not given alms; and their poverty justifies them. There are more saints who have not chastised the body with the austerity of fasting or hair shirts and the weakness of their own constitution excuses them. There are more saints who were not virgins; for so their calling has disposed. But in heaven there is no saint who has not been humble. Has God cast out the Angels from heaven because they were proud, and shall we claim to enter it if we do not keep ourselves in due humility? Without humility, says

San Pier Damiani (*Sermo* 45), neither the Virgin Mary herself with her incomparable virginity would have entered the blessed glory of Christ and we must be convinced of this truth, that without some other virtues we can still be saved, but not already without humility. There are some who think they can do a great deal by keeping chastity unsullied in themselves; and this is really a beautiful frieze; but more than virginity, the Angelic St. Thomas teaches (In 4 dist. 33, quaest. 3, art. 3, ad 6) that humility can be estimated. How rarely is diligence and caution used against spiritual vices, of which the first is pride, and it is the worst of all, which alone sufficed to transform the angel into a demon" (Gaetano da Bergamo, *L'umiltà del cuore*).

"Humility must be part of truth and not of falsehood" (St. Augustine, *De natura et gratia*, 34). The practice of humility must continue throughout our life, since we never get to the point of saying that we have achieved it. Therefore, as long as we live, we must work hard to acquire humility, nor must we ever imagine that we have acquired it; and even if we have it in some degree, we must nevertheless, to preserve it, we must work hard to acquire it, as if we did not have it. The whole rule of Christian wisdom consists in genuine and voluntary humility. It is the foundation of faith. It is the root of all other virtues, as pride is the source of all sin. Humility is the mother, nurturer, support, and anchor of true piety. All the good works are worth nothing unless humility assures them. The lowest place in this world is for this very reason the highest in humility.

Christian humility is a mirror of the most beautiful reality that God created, a mirror of grace. St. Augustine, the teacher of grace, says that God forgives us even the sins we have not committed; He forgives them in the sense that with His grace He prevents us from committing them. "There is no sin committed by one that another cannot commit, if the guidance of God, who made man, is lacking" (*Serm.* 99,6). True Christian humility is revealed in an ever-repentant heart: *cor semper poenitens*, which is a constant loving repentance in our heart. St. Teresa of the Child Jesus, the Saint of the way of spiritual infancy, and an excellent teacher of humility, said: "The only thing that is not envied is the last place, so there is only this last place which is not vanity and spiritual affliction. Therefore, let us humbly place ourselves among the imperfect, let us consider ourselves little souls whom the good Lord must support every time; as soon as He sees us convinced of our nothingness, He stretches out his hand to hold us" (*Letter* 243).

The new edition of the book *The Practice of Humility* by Pope Leo XIII), launched by the *Sensus Fidelium Press*, is therefore of a timeless importance for a true Christian life, especially in our day, where the vice of pride seems to dominate the live of society and even within the Church. May this book bring abundant spiritual fruits to all its readers and help to spread not only the knowledge of true humility, but also the practice of this virtue as the surest, the royal, way to heaven. If there would be another way, God would have shown it to us. But there isn't another way. Since, on which preceded us Our Lord Jesus Christus Himself, His Immaculate and most humble Mother Mary, and every Saint.

+ Athanasius Schneider,
Auxiliary Bishop of Saint Mary in Astana

Preface

CARDINAL NEWMAN, when speaking in the Birmingham Oratory last January, on the occasion of the Papal Jubilee, said: "The Holy Father lived a long life before he became Pope, and little was known of him, yet he has now in the few years that he has become Pope done things which it may be said no other man could do. I scarcely suppose that any of you here present had heard his name before he was made Pope. There did not seem any likelihood that he would ever leave Perugia, his bishopric, but he was found—as others have been found—by a special providence and inspiration of God, and we in our ignorance knew nothing of him."

This golden treatise on *The Practice of Humility*, from the pen of the reigning Sovereign Pontiff, now presented to the English public, comes then as a revelation, and lifts the veil which hitherto has concealed from view the long years of his comparative seclusion spent in Perugia. It shows us the work divine grace was achieving in his heart during that time of his "hidden life" of unconscious preparation for the tiara, and teaches us the school in which his grand character and lofty genius were formed and mellowed. While delineating the humility which those aspiring to perfection should aim at, it in reality presents us with a beautiful portrait of the Holy Father himself, and brings us in touch with his very spirit. For to use the words which St. Gregory the Great wrote of St. Benedict: "So holy a man could by no means teach otherwise than as he lived"—*Sanctus vir nullo modo potuit aliter docere quam vixit.*[1]

Those who have been compelled by duty to renounce the gratification of a pilgrimage to the Eternal City for the Papal Jubilee and to remain at home—those thousands of loyal sons and daughters of holy Mother Church scattered up and down the United Kingdom, in town and hamlet, in the noble house and the humble cottage—one and all, in reading this little work, will acquire a more familiar and intimate acquaintance with the Supreme Pastor of their souls than they could possibly enjoy by merely gazing upon his face and hearing his voice. By it the reader will be drawn under the spell and fascination of his vigorous intellect and striking eloquence, and led to exclaim:—*"Are not his words as a fire, and as a hammer that breaketh the rock in pieces?"*[2]

Though dedicated to his Seminarists[3], the book will be found very suitable to all classes and conditions of men. Is there not reason to think it will even be so cherished by the faithful as to rank with the "IMITATION" and the "SPIRITUAL COMBAT?" So true to life are its admonitions, so profound and searching its lessons, that throughout the Holy Father seems to speak as the spiritual director of every individual soul, as the physician of each human heart, and as the Good Shepherd seeking out the lost sheep. That one so well versed in the secrets of the interior life, and so fully acquainted with the sufferings of poor humanity, should place his finger upon

---

[1]   Dialog. lib. 2. cap. 36.

[2]   Jer. 23:29.

[3]   This book was written by Pope Leo XIII when he was still Joachim Cardinal Pecci, Bishop of Perugia. He wrote this work primarily for his seminarians, but this work can inspire all peoples.

The Practice of Humility as the crying want of the age, and as the most necessary exercise towards the formation of an ascetic priesthood, is not unnatural. For as our blessed Lord by His cross and by His humility drew all men unto Himself, so by the use of these same potent means will His Vicegerents upon earth ever continue to fulfil their glorious and divine mission in the world.

To those outside the fold, who, recognizing the versatility and grasp of his master mind, have been hitherto accustomed to regard him merely as the finished scholar, and the acute philosopher, the great statesman and the arbiter of the nations, this book will reveal the secret which raised him to his present matchless glory—and withal that sustains him in it.

No thoughtful Christian will doubt that the true and supernatural explanation of all those achievements and triumphs may be traced to his humility of spirit. In fact, the Sovereign Pontiff pointed out this truth himself in those memorable, and, as it were, prophetic words spoken in reply to the address of the Sacred College on the day of his coronation, March 3, 1878:—"'Convinced that the most merciful God is He Who chooses the weak things of this world to confound the strong, We live in the certainty that He will sustain Our weakness, and raise up Our lowliness in order to show forth His power and make His strength to shine."

In conclusion, His Holiness has embellished this treatise with a rich appendix of various thoughts culled from spiritual writers, and preceded by the sermon of the great Bishop of Hippo upon the "Fear of God and True Humility." On confronting in their originals St. Benedict's immortal chapter on *Humility* with the discourse of St. Augustine, it is quite perceptible that this must have been a source from which the

Monastic Legislator drew his inspirations, using as he does in one place its very words and expressions. It may be interesting to know that fourteen hundred years later, another Light and Law-giver of the Church repaired to the same fountain. For at the audience in which the Pope graciously accorded permission for the present translation, he condescended to enter upon the motives which led him to compose this valuable treatise, avowing that it was this very sermon of St. Augustine which had inspired him with its first conception.

Joseph Jerome Vaughan, O.S.B.
Monte Cassino, Whitsuntide, 1888.

A Short Biography of Pope Leo Xiii

BORN Gioacchino Vincenzo Raffaele Luigi Pecci on March 2, 1810 in Carpineto Romano (37 miles southeast of Rome), he was elected the 256th pope on February 20, 1878. The sixth of seven sons, Vincenzo would take the name Pope Leo XIII. He was the thirteenth pope to take the name Leo. He wrote eighty-five encyclicals, including eleven on the Rosary. He wrote the St. Michael Prayer following a vision after Holy Mass involving Satan. This little work, *The Practice of Humility*, was written while he was the Bishop of Perugia.

Introduction

THE FOUNDATION OF CHRISTIAN PERFECTION, according to the common teaching of the holy fathers, is humility. "In order to become great," says St. Augustine, "it is necessary to begin by being little. You are desirous of building up the edifice of Christian virtues: know ye then that it is of an immense height. Endeavour, therefore, at once to lay its foundations very deep in humility; for he who is about to erect a building, first of all digs out the foundations in proportion to the bulk and height of the intended structure."[4]

Now this little treatise, which we[5] dedicate to you, O dearly beloved sons, teaches you THE PRACTICE OF HUMILITY that is, it teaches you to lay the foundations of Christian perfection. Think, then, of what great importance it must be to you who are bound to observe in a special manner that commandment of Jesus Christ, *be ye perfect, as your heavenly Father is perfect.* For this reason we feel sure that we are making you a gift which will prove exceedingly dear to you, not only from its being a fresh token of the love We bear you, but also because it will be a most efficacious means towards the salvation of your souls—that most important of all the works in which you may be engaged.

---

[4]   Ser. St. Aug. 10. de Ver. Dom.
[5]   Here the Cardinal uses "we," perhaps referring to himself and those priests responsible for instructing the seminarians.

Also another motive has induced us to address this little book to you: namely, the object of the ecclesiastical state which you have embraced. This object does not merely include your own sanctification, but also the promotion of that of others, by enlarging the kingdom of Jesus Christ through those very same means which He made use of when on earth, for humility of heart was His distinctive characteristic.

This same means will enable you to subdue the pride of the world, and to implant in the hearts of all men the mortification and the humility of the Cross. Since Jesus Christ did not teach until He had first practiced, you also, following His example, should enter upon the sacred ministry already well grounded in THE PRACTICE OF HUMILITY. From this interior and inexhaustible fountain of all virtues will flow forth words of comfort, encouragement, and zeal, whereby to establish the just in sanctity, and to recall those who have gone astray from the paths of vice and perdition into those of virtue and salvation.

Let each one of you in particular, then, be that scholar, who in this little treatise which we dedicate to you, imagines himself to be receiving from his spiritual master lessons on THE PRACTICE OF HUMILITY, and always remember, dear sons, that there is no greater consolation you can give us than that of seeing you humble, meek, and obedient. Trusting, then, that we shall always find you to be such, and in the ardent desire we have that you be so verily and indeed, We bless you all in the Lord, not, however, without once more earnestly exhorting you to use every endeavour to carry out all that this little treatise shall counsel you to practice.

*Joachim Cardinal Pecci, Bishop of Perugia*6

---

6   Joachim Cardinal Pecci took the name Pope Leo XIII when he was elected supreme pontiff on February 20, 1878. He served as pope until his death on July 20, 1903.

Prologue

IT IS AN INCONTROVERTIBLE TRUTH that the proud will meet with no mercy: that the gates of the kingdom of Heaven will be closed against them, and that the Lord will open those gates to none but the *Humble*. To be convinced of this we need simply open Holy Scripture. There we are taught in almost every page, that God resists the proud; that He humbles those who exalt themselves; that we must become like unto little children if we would enter into His glory; that we shall be excluded from it unless we bear this resemblance: in fine, that God pours forth His graces upon none but the humble.

Such being the case we cannot be too strongly impressed of what importance it is for all Christians, and more especially for those who embrace the ecclesiastical state, to endeavor to practice humility, and banish from their minds all presumption, all vanity, all pride.

To secure success in a work so holy no effort or labor should be spared; and as this cannot be attained without the grace of God, we must ask it of Him earnestly and very frequently. Every Christian has contracted in holy Baptism the obligation of walking in the footsteps of Jesus Christ. He is the divine Model to which we should conform our lives. Now in order to humble exaltation and heal the wound of our pride, our Blessed Redeemer carried humility to such a degree as to become the reproach of the world, thereby teaching us through His own example the one road that leads to heaven. The most important lesson taught us by our Savior is, strictly speaking, this: *Learn of Me. Discite a Me.*

Therefore, O disciple of this divine Master, if you would secure this most precious pearl, than which there is no surer pledge of sanctity or more certain token of predestination, receive with docility the counsels which I give you, and faithfully carry them out into practice.

PART I

60 Counsels For Acquiring Humility

1.

OPEN the eyes of your soul and consider that of your own you have nothing that is good by which to pride yourself upon being something.

Of your own you have nothing but sin, weakness, and misery, and with regard to those gifts of nature and of grace which you enjoy, as you have received them from God, Who is the principle of your being, so to Him alone is their glory due.

2.

THEREFORE, be deeply imbued with the idea of your own nothingness, endeavoring to increase it continually in your heart, in spite and to the shame of the pride that lords it over you.

Be intimately persuaded that there is nothing in the world so utterly vain and ridiculous as to wish to be highly esteemed on account of certain endowments which you have received merely as a loan from the gratuitous bounty of the Creator: for as the Apostle says:—"*If thou hast received them, why dost thou glory as though they were thine, and as if thou hadst not received them.*"[7]

3.

FREQUENTLY ponder upon your weakness, your blindness, your vileness, your hard-heartedness, your inconsistency, your sensuality, your insensibility towards God, your attachment to creatures, and upon a host of other vicious inclinations that spring from your corrupt nature.

Let this be to you a strong motive for continually diving deeper into your own nothingness, and for always appearing utterly small and vile in your own eyes.

4.

LET the recollection of the sins of your past life remain ever imprinted on your mind.

Above all things be thoroughly convinced that the sin of pride is an evil so abominable, that any other, be it on the earth above, or in hell beneath, is as nothing in comparison.

This was the sin which made the angels in heaven prevaricate, and that cast them headlong into hell; this it was that corrupted the whole human race and brought upon the earth an infinitude of evils, which will endure as long as the world endures, or rather as long as eternity.

Besides, a soul laden with sin is only worthy of hatred, contempt, and punishment. Imagine, therefore, what possible kind of esteem you can have of yourself—you who have already been guilty of so many sins.

---

[7]   1 Cor. 4:7.

5.

CONSIDER, moreover, that there is no crime, however enormous or deplorable it may be, to which your corrupt nature does not incline, and of which you may not become guilty; and that it is only through the mercy of God, and the help of His grace, that you have been preserved from it up to the present, according to that saying of St. Augustine, "There is no sin in the world which one man has fallen into, which another may not commit, should the hand which created man fail to uphold him."[8]

Weep in your heart over so deplorable a state, and firmly resolve to reckon yourself one of the most unworthy of sinners.

6.

REFLECT frequently that you must sooner or later die, and that your body will have to rot in the grave.

Keep constantly before your eyes the inexorable judgment-seat of Jesus Christ, to which we must all necessarily appear.

Meditate upon the eternal torments of hell, prepared for the wicked, and more especially for those who are most like unto Satan—the proud.

Ponder seriously how, owing to the impenetrable veil that conceals the divine judgments from mortal eye, you are absolutely uncertain whether or not you will be of the number of those reprobates who, in the society of demons, will be cast forever into that place of woe, to be undying victims of a fire enkindled by the very breath of the divine wrath.

---

[8] Solil. c. 15.

This uncertainty should be of itself enough to keep you in a state of the utmost humility, and inspire you with a salutary fear.

7.

DO not flatter yourself that you will ever be able to acquire humility, unless you do practice those particular exercises which are conducive to it.

Acts of meekness, for instance, of patience, of obedience, of mortification, of self-hatred, of the renunciation of your own feelings and opinions, of sorrow for your sins, and the like.

Because these are the only weapons which will destroy in you the earth of self-love, that abominable soil which germinates all your vices, and wherein your pride and presumption take root and spread out in luxuriant growth.

8.

AS far as you are able, preserve silence and recollection, but at all times endeavour to do so without inconveniencing others.

When you are obliged to speak, always do so with reserve, and with modesty and simplicity.

And should it happen that no attention be paid to you, whether out of contempt or from any other cause, do not show any resentment, but accept the humiliation, and bear it with resignation and tranquillity.

9.

MOST diligently guard against and carefully avoid giving utterance to disdainful and haughty expressions, displaying an assumption of superiority, as well as to all studied phrases, and every kind of frivolous jest.

Be ever silent on such matters as might lead others to believe you to be clever and intellectual, and well worthy of their esteem. In a word, never talk of yourself without good reason, nor desire to speak of things calculated to bring upon you honor and praise.

10.

IN your conversation abstain from such observations and sarcastic remarks as may give pain to others; in a word, avoid all that savors of the spirit of the world.

Seldom speak of spiritual matters in a magisterial tone or as one giving advice, unless your charge or charity obliges you to do so.

Speak only of these things in order to be instructed by one who understands such matters, and whom you know to be capable of giving you seasonable advice; for to pose as a master in things spiritual without necessity, is to add fuel to the burning fire—that is to one's soul, which is already ablaze with pride.

11.

REPRESS to the best of your ability all vain and useless curiosity, and be not over-anxious to see what worldlings call things of rarity, beauty, and splendor.

Study rather to know your duty, and what is conducive to your perfection and salvation.

12.

BE always very exact and attentive in treating your superiors with the greatest respect and reverence, your equals with esteem and courtesy, and your inferiors with charity.

Take it for granted that any other behavior is the sure sign of a soul ruled by pride.

13.

FOLLOWING the maxims of the Holy Gospel, always seek the lowest place, thoroughly convinced that such is precisely what befits you.

So also, in all the requirements of life, beware lest your desires and cares should embrace too much and aspire too high.

Be satisfied rather with simple and humble things, as being better suited to your own littleness.

14.

IF earthly consolations fail you, and if God withdraws all spiritual sweetnesses, remember that you have ever abundantly enjoyed them beyond your deserts, and rest satisfied with the way in which the Lord deals with you.

15.

CULTIVATE unceasingly within your soul the pious custom of accusing, reproaching, and condemning yourself.

Judge all your own actions severely, being as they truly are nearly always accompanied with a thousand defects and with the continual arrogance of self-love.

Often conceive a just contempt of yourself, seeing how much thou art wanting in prudence, simplicity, and purity of heart in all your actions.

16.

BEWARE, as of a most grievous evil, of condemning the actions of others, but interpret their every word and deed leniently, seeking with industrious charity for reasons to excuse and defend them.

Should the fault committed be so evident as to allow no opening for defense, strive to attenuate it as far as may be, attributing it to inattention, surprise, or to some such similar cause, according to circumstances.

At all events, think no more of it, unless by reason of your office you are obliged to apply a remedy.

17.

NEVER contradict anyone in conversation, when the point under discussion is an open question, and when there is as much to be said for it as against.

Do not get over-excited in arguing, but if your opinion be considered erroneous or of little worth, give way quietly and then humbly remain silent.

Yield also and behave in like manner with respect to matters of no consequence even when you are satisfied of the mistake of that which has been asserted.

On all other occasions when it is of importance to defend the truth, do so courageously, but without being violent or contemptuous.

Rest assured that you will more likely win by gentleness than by your impetuosity and resentment.

18.

BE well on your guard against giving pain, either by word, action, or in your manner to anyone, however much he may be beneath you, unless you should be at times constrained to do so by duty, obedience, or charity.

19.

SHOULD there be anyone who is continually coming in and out, and pestering you, and making it his business on every occasion to insult you with outrage and injury, yield not to feelings of anger, but look upon him as an instrument which God in His mercy takes use of for your good, so as to heal the inveterate wound of your pride.

20.

THE passion of anger, which derives its violence from that very pride wherein it is rooted, is a vice not to be tolerated in anyone, much less in religious persons.

Endeavor, therefore, to lay up a good store of gentleness, so that should anyone insult you, and wound your feelings with injuries, be they never so grievous, you may still have strength enough to retain your equanimity.

And take great care lest in such cases you nourish or harbor in your heart feelings of dislike and revenge against the person who has offended you; yea, rather forgive him from your heart, being convinced that you can have no better disposition than this for obtaining pardon of those injuries which you have committed even against God Himself.

Be assured that such humble forbearance will earn for you an abundant harvest of merit in Heaven.

21.

BE kind and patient in bearing with the defects and weaknesses of others, keeping always before your eyes your own miseries, by reason of which you also are in need of being borne with and compassionated by others.

22.

IN a word, show humility and meekness towards all, but more especially towards those for whom you feel some repugnance and aversion, avoiding the exclamation which some persons make:—"God forbid that I should entertain any hatred against that man, but I cannot abide his being near me, nor do I care to have anything at all to do with him."

Take it for granted that this dislike arises also from pride, and from you not having conquered haughty nature and self-love with the weapons of grace.

For if these persons would truly abandon themselves to the inspirations of divine grace, they would very soon feel all the difficulties which they experience within themselves overcome by a true humility, and would patiently bear with natures which are even rougher and more uncongenial.

23.

SHOULD any affliction overtake you, bless the Lord, Who has so ordained it for your greater good.

Believe that you have deserved it, and even more and greater troubles, and are not worthy of any consolation.

You may ask the Lord in all simplicity to deliver you from it, if such be pleasing unto Him, otherwise beg Him to give you strength to bear your trial meritoriously.

In your crosses seek not for exterior consolation, especially when it is evident that God sends them to you for your humiliation, and to abate your pride and presumption; but exclaim with the royal Psalmist:—*"It is good for me, O Lord, that Thou hast humbled me, that I may learn Thy justifications."*[9]

24.

FOR the same reason yield not to feelings of annoyance and disgust at table, because the food set before you is little suited to your taste.

Do in this case as the poor of Jesus Christ, who willingly eat whatever is set before them, giving thanks unto Providence.

25.

IF anyone blames or speaks ill of you unjustly, or if your conduct be censured by one who is either your inferior, or who, being more deserving of reprehension than yourself, should look to his own shortcomings, I would not have you on that account fly into a passion, or fling aside the counsels which I have given you, and refuse to examine your conduct in the light of God—and this, from the intimate persuasion that you

---

[9]   Ps. 118:71.

are liable to go astray at every step if the grace of the Lord did not preserve you.

26.

NEVER wish to be singularly loved: for as love depends upon the will, and as the will by its nature tends to that which is good, it follows that to be loved and to be considered good are one and the same thing.

But the desire of being considered exceptionally good, and being esteemed above others, cannot be reconciled with true humility.

O! what great fruit you might derive from acting up to this doctrine!

For your soul, yearning then no longer for the love of creatures, would hide itself in the sacred wounds of its Savior.

There, in the adorable Heart of her Jesus, she would experience ineffable divine sweetness, because having generously renounced the love of creatures for His sake, she would be able to taste abundantly that honey of divine consolation, which would be denied her were she taken up with the false and deceitful sweetnesses of earthly consolations.

For divine consolation is so pure and real that it will not suffer the admixture of that which is earthly; and we are replenished with the one in proportion as we feel disgust for the other.

Moreover, your soul will be able to turn herself freely to God, and by the thought of His presence and infinite perfections to abide in His enjoyment.

Finally, as there is nothing more delightful than to love and be loved, so if you deprive yourself of this pleasure for the love of God, and in order that He may possess your heart whole and undivided, you offer a most acceptable sacrifice to God, and one that is in the highest degree meritorious.

Nor fear lest by so doing your love for your neighbor should grow cold; yea you will rather love him with a purer and more perfect love, loving him no longer out of self-interest, that is for the gratification of your own inclinations, but purely for the sake of pleasing God, and of doing that which you know to be acceptable to Him.

27.

PERFORM all your actions, be they never so trifling, with great attention and the utmost exactness and diligence, because doing them thoughtlessly and hastily is the result of presumption.

The truly humble man is always upon his guard, fearing lest there should be something amiss even in his smallest actions.

For the same reason you should always prefer to practice ordinary exercises of piety, and shun in general all such extraordinary things as your own inclination may suggest to you.

For as the proud man always seeks to make himself singular, so the humble man finds his delight in practices which are common and ordinary.

28.

KNOW that you are not fit to be your own counsellor, and therefore should fear and be diffident of your own opinions as proceeding from a source that is marred and corrupt.

Under this conviction you will, as far as it is possible, always take counsel of some wise and conscientious person, and prefer rather to be led by one better than yourself than to follow your own devices.

29.

WHATEVER high degree of grace and virtue you have attained; whatever gift of prayer God has bestowed upon you, let it be as sublime as you will; even if your life has been one of a thousand years spent in innocence and fervor of devotion— you ought, nevertheless, to walk always in fear and self-distrust, and more especially in matters touching purity.

Recollect that you carry about in you an indestructible germ and an inexhaustible fountain of sin, and know that you are all weakness, all unstableness, all unfaithfulness.

Look, therefore, always to yourself: close your eyes and ears so as neither to see nor hear anything that might sully your soul.

Always shun dangerous occasions, and with the other sex avoid all useless conversations, and in those that are necessary, maintain the most scrupulous modesty and reserve.

Lastly, as you can do nothing good without the grace of God, beg of Him constantly to have mercy on you, and not for a single instant to leave you to yourself.

30.

HAVE you perchance received great talents from God, or are you perhaps famous in the world for some great achievement? Then do you, for this very reason, endeavor the more to know yourself as you truly are, and seek by careful introversion to convince yourself of your own weakness, of your own incapacity, and of your own nothingness.

You ought to appear in your own eyes less than a little child, and not to take delight in the praises of men, and to beware of being ambitious of honor: yea, rather you should always reject both the one and the other.

31.

SHOULD you sustain any grievous injury or meet with some keenly felt disappointment, instead of being indignant against him who has offended you, lift up your eyes to Heaven and fix them upon the Lord, Who in His infinite and loving Providence has so ordained it, either for the expiation of your sins, or to destroy in you the spirit of pride, reducing you to practice acts of patience and humility.

32.

WHEN you meet with an opportunity of rendering your neighbor some lowly and menial service, do so with joy, and with that humility which you would have were you the servant of all.

By this practice you will lay up in store for yourself treasures of virtue and grace.

33.

BUSY not yourself in the least about things which do not in any way concern you, and of which you are not called upon to give an account either to God or to man.

For meddling comes of secret pride and from vain presumption; it nourishes and increases vanity, and begets an infinite host of troubles, worries, and distractions; whereas, by attending to one's self alone and to one's own duties, a man will find a fountain of peace and tranquillity, according to that beautiful saying of *The Imitation of Christ*: "Neither busy thyself with things not committed to thy care, and thus may it be brought about that thou shalt be little or seldom disturbed."[10]

34.

WHEN you perform some extraordinary mortification, take good care to keep free from the venom of vain glory, which oftentimes mars the whole merit.

Take care, I say, to perform it for this sole reason—that it is not becoming in you, since you are so great a sinner, to live at your own ease and pleasure, and because you have so many defects and debts to make satisfaction for in the sight of the divine justice.

Reflect that as the bit and bridle are necessary to master a mettlesome horse, so works of penance are necessary for you in order to check the violence of your passions and keep you within the bounds of duty.

35.

EVERY time you are inclined to be impatient or downcast in your tribulations and humiliations, courageously fight against such a temptation, being mindful of your sins, for which you have deserved far severer chastisements than those from which you are actually suffering.

Adore the infinite justice of God, and with reverence receive its blows, which you should regard as so many fountains of mercy and of grace.

---

[10] B. 3. ch. 25.

Oh! if you could but understand how salutary it is to be smitten in this miserable life by the hand of so sweet a Father as God is, you would then, without doubt, abandon yourself wholly and entirely into His hands.

Frequently cry out with St. Augustine:—"Here in this life, O Lord, burn within me, and cut whatsoever Thou pleasest; here spare me not, provided Thou dost spare and pardon me in eternity."

To refuse tribulations is to rebel against the justice of God, which is so salutary; it is also to reject that chalice which He offers us in His mercy, and which Jesus Christ Himself, although innocent, desired to be the first to drink.

36.

IF by any chance you have committed some fault which has caused you to be despised by the person who witnessed it, conceive a lively sorrow for your offense against God, and for the bad example given to your neighbor; but, with regard to the contempt itself, and the dishonor incurred, accept them as a means which God has chosen for the expiation of your fault, and to render you more humble and more virtuous.

If, on the contrary, seeing yourself depreciated and dishonored mortifies and pains you, believe me, you do not possess true humility, and are still infected with pride.

In this case, all the more earnestly implore the Lord to heal and save you; for if God be not moved to pity towards you, you shall certainly fall into other abysses.

37.

IF among your companions there be one who seems to you contemptible and of no account, you will act wisely and prudently in setting about to consider the good qualities of nature and of grace with which God has endowed him and on account of which he may appear worthy of respect and honor, rather than in noticing his faults and censuring them.

At least, always behold in him one created by God, formed after the divine image and likeness, and redeemed by the precious Blood of Jesus Christ; a Christian illuminated by the light of God's countenance, a soul capable of seeing and possessing God for all eternity, and perhaps one even predestined in the secret counsels of His adorable Providence.

And do you then know the graces which the Lord has already poured out upon his heart, or is about to pour out upon it?

But without troubling yourself about such questions, it would perhaps be better to drive away immediately all those thoughts of contempt as the poisoned breath of the tempter.

38.

WHEN you are praised, instead of rejoicing thereafter, fear lest such praise be the sole reward of that little good which you have done.

In your heart acknowledge your own misery by which you merit the contempt of others, and endeavor to cut short that discourse; not indeed with a view of securing still greater praise—like the proud, who make a parade of humility—but with a holy adroitness, so that attention may be wholly drawn away from you.

But if in this you do not succeed, instantly refer to God alone all the honor and all the glory, saying with Baruch and Daniel:—*"To the Lord our God belongeth justice, but to us confusion of our face."*[11]

39.

AS your own praises should give you disgust, so in the same degree ought the praises conferred upon others to cause you delight: and do you also contribute your mete of praise so far as sincerity and truth will permit.

The envious cannot endure the glory bestowed upon their neighbour, because they regard it as so much taken from their own.

For this very reason they adroitly let fall in their conversations certain half finished thoughts and ambiguous phrases, either to lessen or cast doubt on the praises which they hear conferred upon others.

Not thus should you act; but in praising your neighbor praise and thank the Lord for the gifts He has bestowed upon him, and for the services which He receives at his hands.

40.

WHEN your neighbor is defamed in your hearing, conceive a sincere sorrow for it.

Seek in your mind for some motive whereby to excuse the weakness of the detractor.

Do not fail, however, to defend the honor and good name of the poor person who is the object of attack, doing so with

---

[11] Bar. 1:15.

such skill and tact that the defense shall not turn out to be in reality a second accusation.

Thus, for example, at times try and touch upon his praiseworthy qualities, or put in a clear light how highly he is esteemed by others as well as by yourself; at times endeavour to change in a skilful way the subject of conversation, or let it be in some way understood how distasteful it is to you.

By acting thus, you will confer the utmost benefit upon yourself, the detractor, the bystanders, and the person maligned.

But if without making the slightest effort to repress your feelings, you do feel pleased you're your neighbor is depreciated, and when he is extolled, displeased, O then, how much still remains for you to do before possessing the incomparable treasure of humility.

41.

THERE is nothing more conducive to your spiritual advancement than to be told of your faults.

Hence it is very expedient and necessary that you should encourage those who sometimes have done you this service that they may continue to do so on every occasion.

Since you have received their admonitions with joy and gratitude, make it your duty to put them into practice, and this, not only because of the advantage which self-correction brings with it, but also in order to show to these faithful friends that their care of you has not been in vain, and that you are extremely sensible of their kindness.

The proud man, even when he corrects himself, does not wish it to appear that he is following the salutary counsels which he has received of others; nay, he even shows a supreme contempt for them.

But the truly humble man glories in submitting himself to all persons for the love of God, and looks upon the wise admonitions he receives as coming from God Himself, without reflecting upon the instrument which is made use of.

42.

ABANDON yourself entirely to God in order to follow the dispensations of His loving Providence, even as a tender child casts itself without reserve into the arms of its beloved father.

Let God do with you whatsoever He pleases, without disturbing or disquieting yourself about anything that may befall you.

With joyfulness, with confidence, and with reverence, accept everything that comes to you from Him.

To act otherwise, would be to requite the goodness of His heart with ingratitude—would be to distrust Him!

Humility plunges us infinitely below the infinite Being of God, but at the same time it teaches us that in Him alone is all our strength and every consolation.

43.

SINCE it is clear that without God you are not able to do any good whatsoever, and that you would fall at every step and be overcome by the slightest temptation, always acknowledge yourself to be the weak and impotent creature you are, bearing in mind that in all your actions, you stand continually in need of the divine assistance.

By means of these thoughts keep yourself inseparably united to God, even as the infant clings to the bosom of its mother, knowing of no other secure support.

Say often with the royal Prophet:—"*Unless the Lord had been my helper, my soul had almost dwelt in hell.*"[12] And:—"*Look Thou upon me and have mercy on me, for I am alone and poor.*"[13] And:— "*O God, come to my assistance; O Lord, make haste to help me.*"[14]

Lastly, cease not to give thanks to the Lord with all the outpouring of your heart. Above all things, thank Him for the protection with which He forestalls and encompasses you.

Beg Him constantly to deign to give you those special helps of which you stand in need, and which He alone is able to bestow.

44.

IN the hour of prayer, more especially than at any other time, you should be penetrated with a feeling of shame and confusion and self-abasement, and with a holy awe of the presence of that Supreme Majesty to Whom you do dare appeal:—"*I will speak to the Lord, whereas I am but dust and ashes.*"[15]

If in your prayer you receive some extraordinary favor, you should at once believe yourself to be unworthy of it, and understand that God has bestowed it upon you gratuitously, and out of His pure mercy.

Guard yourself well against imagining that it belongs to you of right, and against taking any vain complacency in it.

And if you do not receive any such signal gift, you should not be on that account cast down.

Rather reflect that much yet remains for you to do before you are worthy of such favors, and that God is exceedingly

---

12   Ps. 93:17.
13   Ps. 24:16.
14   Ps. 69:1.
15   Gen. 27:27.

good and patient even in permitting you simply to lie at His feet, and to be, as it were, like the poor beggar, who waits whole hours at the door of the rich man's house, to obtain some trifling alms wherewith to alleviate his misery.

45.

BE ever most prompt in giving to God the entire glory both of your good deeds and of the happy issue of the undertakings committed to your care.

To yourself attribute nothing except their defects, for these emanate from yourself alone; whereas every good is from God, and to Him only are due the thanks and the glory of every good deed.

Impress this truth so deeply upon your mind as never to forget it.

Believe, that any other person helped by divine grace as you have been, would have succeeded far better than you have done, and would not be guilty of so many imperfections.

Reject the praises which may be offered you for any unexpected success, for they are not due to so vile an instrument as you are; but rather to that immense, sublime, and eternal Master-Builder Who is able, if He has a mind, to make use of a rod to strike water out of the rock, of a little clay to restore sight to the blind, and Who has power to work an infinity of miracles.

46.

IF, on the contrary, the affairs placed under your direction go wrong, it is much to be feared that the failure must be attributed to your incapacity and to your negligence.

Your self-love and your pride, which recoil from every humiliation, would seek perhaps to throw the blame upon others, and when unable to do this, would strive at least to extenuate the fault.

But do not encourage these vicious inclinations. Examine your conduct conscientiously, and trembling lest you have failed in doing your duty, acknowledge your fault before God, and accept the humiliation as a chastisement which you have deserved.

If, however, your conscience does not reproach you, adore even in this case the dispensations of God, and reflect that perhaps your past sins and too much self-confidence have caused the blessing of Heaven to be withdrawn from your labors.

47.

WHEN approaching the most Holy Communion, with a heart all inflamed with divine love, you should at the same time approach with a mind penetrated with sentiments of true humility.

And how could you not be wholly amazed on reflecting that a God, infinitely pure and infinitely holy, entertains such a surpassing degree of love for so miserable a creature as you are, even to the giving you His very Self for food!

Dive as deeply as you can into the abyss of your unworthiness. Draw not nigh to that adorable Sanctity except with the utmost reverence.

And when it shall please that amiable Lord, Who in this Sacrament is all Love, to caress you, communicating Himself to you in the plenitude of His unutterable sweetness, take every

possible precaution against falling away from the reverence due
to His infinite majesty.

Keep yourself always in your proper place: that is, in
submission, in subjection, and in your nothingness.

And yet the sense of your poverty and wretchedness ought
not in any way to produce the effect of closing up your heart,
or of depriving you in the least of that holy confidence which
you should have in this heavenly Banquet.

Nay, it should make you grow in love towards God, Who
humbles Himself to such a degree as to become the nourishment
of your soul.

48.

FOR your neighbor entertain true and living charity, and a
perpetual fountain of affability and sweetness, and seek with
a holy avidity how to help him in all things. But always do so
to please God.

Examine well the motives of your actions, and thus you
shall discover every snare of vanity and self-love.

Refer all the good you do to God alone.

Know that if you keep a good action so hidden and
secret as to be known to none but God, it shall secure you a
priceless reward.

If, however, through your negligence it becomes noised
abroad, then, like a beautiful fruit which the birds have begun
to peck at, it loses almost all its value.

49.

SEEING yourself in continual danger of falling, let that
wholesome fear which you should entertain of displeasing

the Lord, be ever accompanied by an interior sigh towards Him, that His infinite mercy may preserve you from so great a misfortune.

These interior sighs are, in reality, those groanings and yearnings of the heart recommended by the saints, which prompt us to attend to ourselves and to our own actions, to the meditation of divine truths, to the contempt of all things fleeting, to the practice of interior prayer, and to the keeping ourselves estranged from all that is not of God.

In a word, this practice is a fountain of true humility and poverty of spirit.

Make frequent use of it, and as far as in you lies, let it be your continual prayer.

50.

A sick man, who ardently desires to be cured, takes the greatest pains to ward off everything that might retard his progress, eats with the utmost moderation, even the most wholesome food, and considers at almost every mouthful whether it may or may not do him harm.

So, in like manner, if you earnestly desire to be cured of the fatal disease of pride, and if you truly aspire to the precious possession of humility, you must be always attentive and cautious lest you say or do anything which might impede you therein.

And with this object, it will be well on each occasion to ponder whether that which you are about to do, tends or tends not to humility, in order either to do it immediately with joy or to discard it entirely.

51.

ANOTHER exceedingly powerful motive to induce you to practice the beautiful virtue of humility is the example of our Divine Savior, Whom we should continually take as our Model.

He it is Who says to us in the holy Gospel: "*Learn of Me, because I am meek and humble of heart.*"[16]

And, in fact, as St. Bernard remarks: "What pride is there which the humility of this divine Master cannot extinguish?"

Verily it may be said that He alone in reality humbles and abases Himself, and that we, when we seem to humiliate ourselves, do not lower ourselves at all, but simply take the place which belongs to us.

For being vile creatures, guilty perhaps of a thousand misdeeds, we can lay claim to no other right than nothingness and punishment.

But our Savior Jesus Christ, lowered Himself infinitely beneath that lofty height which belongs to Him.

He is the omnipotent God, the infinite and immortal Being, the Supreme Arbiter of all things.

And notwithstanding this, He became man—weak, mortal, subject to suffering, obedient even unto death.

He has borne the lack of all temporal things. He Who in Heaven constitutes the joy and the beatitude of the angels and of the saints, willed to become the "Man of Sorrows," and took upon Himself each and all of the miseries of humanity.

The uncreated Wisdom, and of all wisdom the Principle, has borne the shame and mockery due to a fool.

The Holy of Holies and Sanctity in essence, suffered Himself to be reputed a villain and a malefactor.

---

[16]   Matt. 11:29.

He Whom the countless hosts of the blessed in Heaven adore, willed to die a disgraceful death upon a Cross.

And lastly, He Who by nature is the Sovereign Good, has endured every kind of human misery.

Then, after such an example of humility, what ought we not to do—we who are but dust and ashes!

And what humiliation should ever appear hard to us—to us, who are not only most abject and vile worms, but what is worse still, most miserable sinners.

52.

CONSIDER, moreover, the examples left to you by the saints, both of the Old and the New Covenant. Isaias, that prophet so virtuous and zealous, believed himself to be impure in the sight of God, and openly declared that all his "justices" were as filthy "rags."[17]

Daniel, whom God Himself, in the Book of Ezechiel, describes as a holy man, capable of arresting by his prayers the divine wrath, spoke to God with the humility of a sinner, and as one who ought always to be overwhelmed with confusion and shame.

St. Dominic, a prodigy of innocence and holiness, had attained to such a degree of self-contempt, as to fear lest he should draw down the curse of Heaven upon those cities through which he was obliged to pass.

Therefore, before entering them, he would prostrate with his face to the earth, and weeping, cry out: "I ask You, O my God, through Your most tender mercy, to regard not my sins, lest this city, which is about to suffer me to linger within

---

[17] Isa. 64:6.

its walls, should in consequence feel the effects of Your just vengeance."

St. Francis, who through his purity of life, merited to bear in his body the marks of the Passion of Jesus Christ, firmly and sincerely believed himself to be the most wicked of men.

This persuasion so possessed his mind that no one was ever able by any means to disabuse him of it.

The reason he gave for it was this: that if the least of mankind had received from God all those. signal graces which had been bestowed upon him, such an one would have made far better use of them, and certainly would not have requited them with such base ingratitude.

Various other saints believed themselves unworthy of the food of which they partook, of the air they breathed, of the clothing which covered them.

Others looked upon it as an extraordinary miracle of the divine mercy that they were suffered to remain upon the face of the earth, and were not precipitated headlong into hell.

Others again wondered how their fellow-men could put up with them, and why the whole of creation did not unite as one man to exterminate and annihilate them.

Lastly, the saints have all held in abhorrence dignities, praises, and honors, and from that utmost contempt with which they regarded themselves, we see that they longed for nothing else than humiliations and scorn.

And are you more illuminated or holier than they?

Why not then place, as did these saints, your sole and entire delight in holy humility?

53.

NOW to increase the more in this virtue and render humiliations sweet and familiar, you will find it of great advantage to picture to yourself frequently the affronts which might come upon you unaware, endeavoring, notwithstanding rebellious nature, to accept them as sure pledges of the love of your God and as certain means for your own sanctification.

Perhaps in doing this you may have to undergo many struggles, but act courageously and be valiant in the strife, until you feel yourself firm and resolute to suffer all with joy for the love of Christ.

54.

LET not a day pass in which you reproach not yourself for that for which your enemies might reproach you; and that not only to sweeten beforehand the effect of such reproaches, but more especially to maintain you in a state of lowliness and self-disesteem.

But if it should happen that in the tempest of some violent temptation you are inclined to be impatient and to murmur interiorly at the way in which God tries you, repress these feelings betimes, and say within yourself: "What! should a vile and miserable sinner such as I, dare complain of this tribulation?

"And have I not already deserved punishments infinitely worse?

"Knowest thou not, O my soul, that humiliations and sufferings are indeed my true bread, bestowed upon me as an alms by the Lord, so that I may for once and all rise up out of my misery and want?

"Ah! should you refuse these alms, you are not worthy of them, rejecting as you do so rich a treasure, which perhaps will be taken away from you and given to others to make better use of.

"The Lord wishes to number you among His friends and disciples on Calvary, and would you, yielding to base fear, make 'the great refusal' of combat?[18]

"And how can you expect to be crowned without having fought? And how can you claim your wages when you have not borne the 'burdens of the day and the heats?'"

These and the like reflections will rekindle your fervor, and will beget in you a desire of leading a life, even of suffering and humiliation, in imitation of the life of our Savior Jesus Christ.

55.

HOWEVER great may be the peace and tranquillity which you enjoy in the midst of abuse and contradiction, you should not on that account take it for granted that you possess a calm and triumphant humility, because pride is frequently only dormant, and if it happen to be aroused, it begins anew to inflict upon the soul serious injuries and losses.

Let the study of the knowledge of yourself, the fleeing from honors, and the love of humiliations, be your weapons; and of these you should never divest yourself, no, not even for a single moment.

If thus you shall acquire that rich inheritance of humility, then will you have no longer any fear of losing it, because it is

---

[18] An allusion to *Dante* (*Inferno* iii. 60), where the poet vindictively attributes the abdication—"il gran rifuto"—of Celestine V. (1294) to cowardice, and in consequence places him in that circle of *Hell* inhabited by those disdained alike by justice and mercy.

only by continually humbling yourself that you shall preserve the precious gift of humility.

56.

IN order that God may deign to grant you so great a favor, take for your advocate and protectress the most blessed Virgin.

St. Bernard says, that Mary, more than any other creature, humbled herself, and that being the greatest of all human beings, she, through the most profound abyss of her humility, made herself the least.

For this very reason Mary received the plenitude of grace, and became worthy to be the Mother of God.

At the same time, Mary is a Mother of mercy and tenderness, to whom no one ever has had recourse in vain.

Full of confidence, abandon yourself to her maternal heart. Beseech her to obtain for you that virtue which was so dear to her. Fear not that she will be loath to take this petition under her special care.

No! Mary will demand it for you from God, Who quickens the humble and annihilates the proud.

Moreover, as Mary is all-powerful with her Son, He will certainly grant her request.

Fly to her in all your wants, in all your temptations. Let Mary be your support, let Mary be your consolation.

But the chief grace which you should ask of her is holy humility. Do not hold your peace, neither cease imploring until she has obtained it.

Nor fear being too importunate.

O! how pleasing to Mary is this importunity to obtain the salvation of your soul, and to render yourself more acceptable to her Divine Son.

Lastly, that you may induce her to be more and more favorable and propitious, conjure her by her own humility, which was the cause of her elevation to the dignity of Mother of God, and by her divine maternity, which was the ineffable fruit of her humility.

57.

FOR the same reason, you should also have recourse to those saints in whom this pre-eminent virtue has shone forth the most conspicuously.

For instance, to St. Michael the Archangel, who was the first of the humble, as Lucifer was the first of the proud.

To St. John the Baptist, who having attained to so sublime a degree of sanctity as to be taken for the Messiah, nevertheless had so mean an opinion of himself that he thought he was unworthy even to loose the latchet of His shoes.

To St. Paul, that privileged Apostle, who was rapt up to the third heavens, and who, after having heard the innermost secrets of the Divinity, regarded himself as the least of the Apostles, and even unworthy of the name of an Apostle, and to be, as it were, a mere *nothing*.[19]

To St. Gregory, Pope, who took more pains to escape the Supreme Pontificate of the Church than the ambitious take to secure the highest honors.

To St. Augustine, who in the height of his fame, and extolled by all his contemporaries, both as a holy Bishop and as the most acute Doctor of the Catholic Church, left to the whole world in those two marvellous books of his—the

---

[19] 2 Cor. 12:11.

"Confessions" and "Retractations"—immortal monuments of his humility.

To St. Alexius, who, within the walls of his paternal home, preferred the insults and ill-treatment of his very servants, to all the honors and dignities which he might so easily have obtained.

To St. Aloysius Gonzaga, who, lord and marquess of a vast estate, renounced it with joy, and in preference to a grand position in the world, chose a life of humility and mortification.

In a word, you should have recourse to those other numerous saints, who by reason of their humility, shine with a most brilliant lustre in the annals of the Church.

Rest assured, that these humble servants of God will intercede for you before His throne in Heaven, that you also may attain to being of the number of the faithful imitators of their virtue.

58.

LASTLY, the drawing nigh frequently to the sacraments of Penance and Communion, will supply most abundant aid to maintain you in the practice of humility.

Confession, in which we reveal to a fellow-creature all the most secret and shameful miseries of our souls, is the greatest act of humiliation which Jesus Christ enjoined upon His disciples.

Holy Communion, by which we receive within our breasts in very substance the God made man and annihilated for love of us, is a wonderful school of humility and a most powerful means of acquiring it.

How can you doubt but that your amiable Jesus desires to communicate this virtue of humility to you when His Sacred

Heart, that Heart so meek and humble, that furnace of love and charity, is reposing, as it were, upon your own heart, and your heart asks it of Him with all the fervour of its affections.

Approach as frequently as you are able to receive this adorable Sacrament; and provided that you do bring unto It the necessary dispositions, you shall always find in It that *hidden manna* reserved for him only who seeks It with great eagerness.

59.

FOR the rest, always take courage in overcoming the difficulties you shall encounter in practicing what I have taught you thus far, and in resisting the opposition which you shall find within yourself.

Be well on your guard against exclaiming with the faint-hearted disciples: "*This is a hard saying, who can bear it?*"[20]—and who can carry it out into practice?

For of a truth I assure you, that all the bitterness you shall find at the outset, will very quickly be changed into ineffable sweetness and heavenly consolations.

A holy perseverance in these exercises will free you from a thousand torments of soul, and will infuse into your heart so much peace and tranquility that you shall enjoy a foretaste of that eternal happiness which God has prepared in Heaven for His faithful servants.

If, through cowardice you do give up practicing the necessary means to become truly humble, you shall always feel dejected, disquieted, discontented, and be intolerable to yourself, if not also to others; and what is of greater consequence, thou will incur a great risk of being lost eternally.

---

[20] John 6:61.

It is certain, at all events, that the gate of perfection will be closed against you, there being no other door by which you can enter save that of humility.

Strengthen yourself, therefore, with a holy ardour, so that nothing may be able to subdue you. Lift up your eyes on high and there behold Jesus Christ, Who, heavily laden with His cross, teaches you the road of humility and patience, trodden already by so many saints, who are now reigning with Him in Heaven.

Hearken how earnestly He calls upon you to follow the same road taken by Himself and by all the faithful imitators of His virtues.

See how the holy angels all long for your salvation; see how they implore you to enter upon that narrow path, the only safe one, no, the only one which leads to Heaven, and which will conduct you to those thrones of eternal glory left vacant through the pride of the rebel angels.

And do you not already hear the blessed triumphantly proclaiming throughout paradise that by no other road have they come to the possession of that immense glory, than by that of humiliation and of suffering?

See how they rejoice, and how gladsome they are with you for those first desires which you have conceived of imitating their example.

Fortify yourself, therefore, with might and courage to set about this grand work without further delay.

Recall to your mind those most sacred vows you made in your Baptism, and tremble at the mere thought of violating the sanctity of the solemn promises which you did then make to God.

Know, beyond everything else, that Jesus Christ expressly declared, that the *"kingdom of heaven suffereth violence."*[21]

Blessed are you, yea, a thousand times blessed, if, convinced of this truth, you make it your first endeavor to practice humility, that so you may merit the reward of the eternal greatness of Heaven.

60.

IN the last place, reflect that our divine Master exhorted His disciples to acknowledge themselves *unprofitable servants,* even when they had fulfilled all the Commandments.[22]

So should you also acknowledge yourself an unprofitable servant, even after having practiced all the foregoing counsels with the utmost exactness; being firmly convinced that such is not due to your own strength and merits, but indeed to the gratuitous goodness and infinite mercy of God.

Thank Him without ceasing, with all the love and outpouring of your heart, for so great a blessing.

Finally, beseech Him every day to vouchsafe to preserve this priceless treasure within you, even to that very moment when your soul, released from every tie which keeps you bound to creatures, shall be free to wing its flight to the bosom of its Creator, there to enjoy for all eternity the glory prepared for the humble.

---

[21] Matt. 11:12.
[22] Luke 17:10.

PART II

Saints on Humility

SERMON OF ST. AUGUSTINE
On the Fear of God and on True Humility
(*De Tempore*, Serm. ccxii.)

D AVID, the Royal Prophet and Psalmist, who, as the
Scriptures testify, being a man after God's own heart,
performed His every will; this holy Prophet, I say, dearly
beloved brethren, in a certain passage points out to us what it
is that our Creator desires and loves, crying out in these words:
"*Who is as the Lord our God, Who dwelleth on high, and looketh
down upon the low things in heaven and in earth.*"[23]

If, therefore, the Lord Most High, of Whose perfection and
greatness there is no end, regards and welcomes humility in
all His creatures—be they the most exalted or the most lowly,
angels or men—how necessary, therefore, must it be that we
should continually look to humility and practice it always in
everything, in order thus to give pleasure to our Creator.

How great a virtue, then, true humility is, may be gathered
easily from those words of our Savior, Who, to condemn the

---

[23] Ps. 113:5.

pride of the Pharisees, says: "*Everyone that exalteth himself shall be humbled, and he that humbleth himself shall be exalted.*"[24]

It is only by the steps of humility that the heights of Heaven can be reached, for not by means of pride do we mount to God on high, but in truth by humility, according to that which is written: "*God resisteth the proud, and giveth grace to the humble.*"[25] And it is written in the Psalms: "*The Lord is high and looketh on the low, and the high He knoweth afar off.*"[26] Here *the high* signify the proud. He *looketh upon the low* to exalt them, and *knoweth the high afar off*, that is the proud, to cast them down. Let us learn humility in order to enable us to approach the Lord, as He Himself says in the Gospel: "*Learn of Me, because I am meek and humble of heart, and you shall find rest to your souls.*"[27] By pride the once admirable and angelic creature was cast down headlong from Heaven, and by the humility of God human nature ascended thither. Beautiful, even in the sight of men, is the practice of humility, as Solomon declares: "*Where pride is, there also shall be reproach, but where humility is, there also is wisdom.*"[28] Again, another wise man says: "*The greater thou art, the more humble thyself in all things, and thou shalt find grace before God.*"[29] And God Himself says by the mouth of His prophet: "*To whom shall I have respect but to him that is poor and little and of contrite heart, and that trembleth at my words.*"[30]

In one who is not humble and meek the grace of the Holy Spirit can never dwell. God humbled Himself in order to save us. Let man blush to be proud. As profoundly as the heart

---

[24] Luke 14:11.
[25] James 4:6.
[26] Ps. 137:6.
[27] Matt. 11:29.
[28] Prov. 11:2.
[29] Eccles. 3:20.
[30] Isa. 66:2.

abases itself in humility, so high does it rise in perfection: for he who is humble shall be exalted in glory. The first degree of humility is, to hearken humbly to the words of truth, to keep them in memory, to practice them willingly. Truth, certainly, ever flees from a mind which is not humble. The less you are in your own estimation the greater will you be in the sight of God. But the proud man, the more illustrious he appears to be to the world, the more contemptible will he be before God. He who practices all virtues, but with no humility, is like a man who carries dust before the wind. Furthermore, the Scripture cries out: *"And why dost thou exalt thyself, dust and ashes!"*[31] while the wind of pride carries away and scatters all that you imagine yourself to have amassed by fasts and alms.

Be well on your guard, O man, less you make a boast of your virtue; for you shall not yourself be your own judge, but Another, before Whom, strive to keep yourself lowly of heart, in order that He may exalt you in the day of recompense. Descend, therefore, in order to ascend. Humble yourself that you may be exalted, lest having exalted yourself you should be humbled. For he who is unsightly in his own eyes, is beautiful before God. He who is displeasing to himself, is pleasing unto God. Be therefore little in your own eyes, so as to be great in the eyes of God; for the more vile you are in your own estimation, the more precious shall you be in the sight of God. In the highest honors, have the deepest humility. Honor derives its greatest glory from the virtue of humility.

But this virtue of humility no man can have without the fear of God, because the one cannot exist without the other.

Now with regard to the effect of the fear of God, hearken to me, my brethren: *"The beginning of wisdom is the fear of*

---

[31] Eccles. 10:9.

the Lord."[32] The fear of the presence of God is a great preservative against sin. He who perfectly fears God, takes great care to avoid sin. "*With him who feareth the Lord, it shall be well in the latter end,*"[33] and his recompense shall endure forever. If a person be ashamed to transgress before men, how much more commendable and requisite, then, is it that he should be ashamed to commit iniquity in the sight of God, Who looks not only to the deed, but, likewise, to the heart. Those who fear God with a holy fear seek the things that are pleasing to Him. There is the fear of children and there is the fear of servants. Servants fear their masters for the dread of punishment, but children fear for the love of their father. If we be children of God, let us fear Him for the sweetness of charity, not out of the bitterness of fear. The wise man in all his actions fears God, because he knows it is impossible to hide from His presence, according to the words of the Psalmist when addressing God: "*Whither shall I go from Thy spirit, or whither shall I flee from Thy face;*"[34] to which is added, in another place: "*From the east even unto the west there is no hiding-place for him who fleeth from God.*" We who fear the Lord will accept His doctrine, and he who shall be careful to keep His commandments, shall find everlasting benediction. "*The soul of him that feareth the Lord is blessed,*"[35] he abides secure from the temptations of the Evil One. "*Blessed is the man who is always fearful,*"[36] and to whom it is given to have ever before his eyes the fear of God. He who fears the Lord turns aside from the crooked way and

32   Ps. 110:9.

33   Eccles 1:13.

34   Ps. 138:7.

35   Eccles. 34:17.

36   Prov. 28:14.

directs his steps in the path of virtue. *"The fear of the Lord driveth out sin,"*[37] and induces virtue. The fear of God renders man careful and anxious not to sin. But where there is no fear of God there is dissoluteness of life. He who fears not God in prosperity, let him at least fear Him in adversity, and let him fly for succour to Him Who scourges and heals, for: *"Blessed the man that feareth the Lord, and who endeavours with all the desires of his heart to keep His commandments."*[38] The fear of God drives out the fear of hell, because it makes a man avoid sin and multiply his works of justice. After this, he will arrive at that fear which, being founded upon love, is called *"holy, enduring for ever and ever."*[39] Thus, therefore, brethren, Iet us fear God that we may love Him, for perfect charity casts out servile fear, and by this means we shall acquire abundant security and the plenitude of every good. Wherefore the Royal Prophet says: *"Fear the Lord all ye His saints, for there is no want to them that fear Him. The rich have wanted and suffered hunger, but they that seek the Lord shall not be deprived of any good."**

I implore you, therefore, dearly beloved, to keep in view the fear of God; ever in your minds, to strive at all cost not to be unmindful of His precepts, and to consider seriously, that whereas he who fears God and keeps His commandments enters into life everlasting, he who despises Him and rejects His precepts, will go into everlasting torments.

Once more, I beseech you, to nourish interiorly within your hearts true humility, and by its unfeigned practice, to instill it into your neighbours, so that they also, being edified by your good example, may glorify God, and in union with you, strive

---

37 Eccles. 1:27.
38 Ps. 111:1.
39 Ps. 18:10.

to obtain an eternal reward in Heaven, through the help and grace of our Lord Jesus Christ, Who lives and reigns for ever and ever. Amen.

Various Thoughts on Humility

1.

"KNOW, you humble, that our Redeemer "*humbled Himself, becoming obedient unto death.*"[40] Know, you proud, that of your Chief it is written, "*He is king over all the children of pride.*"[41] The beginning of our ruin, then, was the pride of the devil, and the cause of our redemption was the humility of God. For our enemy being created like all other things, wished to appear to be exalted above all; but our Redeemer, the greatest above all things, deigned to become the lowliest of all. Therefore, tell the humble, while they abase themselves they rise to the imitation of God; and tell the proud, while they exalt themselves, they sink down to the imitation of the apostate angel. Is there anything, therefore, more despicable than pride, which, while it exalts itself, recedes from the height of true greatness? Or is there anything more glorious than humility, which, while it stoops to the lowest depths is united to the Most High, its Creator?"

—St. Gregory the Great (*Past. Par. 3. Adm.* 18)

---

[40] Phil. 2:8.
[41] Job 41:25.

2.

"IN nothing can the two virtues of humility and charity be separated. And so inseparable is their connection, that he who is established in the one, is of necessity master of the other. For as humility is a part of charity, so is charity a part of humility. And if we carefully reflect on those works which the Apostle terms fruitless, and of no profit without charity,[42] we shall find that these very same works are sterile if they be devoid of true humility. And of a verity, what fruit can knowledge produce united with conceit; or faith with human glory; or almsgiving with ostentation; or martyrdom with pride? Wherefore, since humility and charity both tend alike to the destruction of pride, what has been said of the one may be also applied to the other."

—St. Ambrose (*Epist. Libr. 10. ad Demetriadem*)

3.

"CHARITY is preserved by means of humility, for there is nothing which destroys it so quickly as pride. Hence the Lord did not say: "*Take up My yoke upon you and learn of Me,*" to raise the dead, who had been in the grave four days; to cast out evil spirits from demoniacs; to heal diseases and work other similar miracles; but He did say: "*Take up My yoke upon you and learn of Me, because I am meek and humble of heart.*"[43] These miracles, indeed, are indications of spiritual things, but to be meek and humble is the preservative of charity."

—St. Augustine (*In exposit. Epist. ad Galatas*)

---

[42] 1 Cor. 13.1-3.
[43] Matt. 11:29.

4.

"HE who knows that he is dust and ashes, and into dust must soon return, will never proudly exalt himself: and he who has pondered upon the eternity of God, and reflects upon that short space, or, so to speak, point of space, which constitutes human life, will ever keep death before his eyes, and be humble and lowly. For this corruptible body weighs down the soul, and our hearts, entangled with so many things, become depressed by this earthly tabernacle. Wherefore, let us say in all humility: "*Lord, my heart is not exalted, nor are my eyes lofty; neither have I walked in great matters, nor in wonderful things above me.*"[44] All true humility, then, is to be sought, not so much in words as in the mind, so that in the innermost conviction of our souls, we should acknowledge ourselves to be nothing; nor ought we ever to imagine ourselves either to know or to understand anything, or to be anything at all."

—St. Jerome (*In exposit. Epist. ad Ephes. cap.* 4)

5.

"MY son, have a care above all things of humility, for this, of all virtues, is the most sublime, and the ladder whereby to reach the summit of perfection.

Good resolutions are not carried into effect save by humility, and the labours of many years are brought to nothing through pride. The humble man is like unto God, and carries Him within the temple of His heart; but the proud man, in being odious to God, bears resemblance to the devil. Although the humble man may appear outwardly loathsome and contemptible, yet he is glorious in his virtues; and,

---

[44] Ps. 130:1.

notwithstanding the loud display of state and dignity the proud man may make in sight of the world, yet his works quickly betray him as a man of no worth. His pride is detected by his gait and every movement, and his levity becomes apparent even in his words. He ever craves after the praises of men, and destitute as he is of all virtues, he goes about pretending to be full of them to the overflow. He cannot bear to be subjected to anyone, but ever aims at pre-eminence above others, and does all in his power to advance to a higher rank. That which he cannot obtain by merit, he endeavors to usurp by ambition. He walks about swelled with conceit, like a bag full of wind, and in all he does shows so much fickleness, that one might take him for a ship, which deprived of its captain, has become the sport of the billows. The humble man, on the contrary, shuns every earthly honor, reckons himself as the least of men, and though to look at, he would be taken to be of little importance, yet he stands eminently high before God. When he has fulfilled all that was commanded him he affirms that he has done nothing, and is most solicitous to conceal every virtue of his soul. But the Lord brings to light all his works, and proclaims them far and wide. He discovers his marvellous deeds to the world. He will exalt him and make him glorious, and in the hour of his prayer, grant him all he shall ask."

—St. Basil the Great *(Admon. ad Fil. Spir)*

6.

"THE poor in spirit are the humble of heart; that is to say, those are called poor in spirit who hold themselves in low estimation. On the contrary, by the rich in spirit is understood the proud, who have a high opinion of themselves, and do not fulfil the commandment of Jesus Christ, which declares that: *"Unless you become as little children, you cannot enter into the kingdom of heaven:*[45] for whosoever has already become as a little child, is poor in spirit, and he who is poor in spirit has indeed become as a little child. And although, according to the testimony of Jesus Christ and of the Apostle,[46] love is the *fulfilment of the law*, yet the nurse of love is humility, and the mother of hatred is pride.

Therefore, humility is the beginning of all good, and the origin of every evil is pride."

—St. John Chrysostom (Parall. Lib. 3. cap. 84)

7.

"BEHOLD wherein consists the *foundation* of humility: to reckon one's self a sinner, and to believe that one has done nothing well in the sight of God. Now, behold wherein consists the *practice* of humility: in the love of silence; in not comparing one's self with others; in not contradicting; in walking in subjection; in observing custody of the eyes; in picturing death to the mind; in abhorring falsehoods; in fleeing unnecessary and idle talk; in not opposing elders; in not being wedded to one's own opinion; in suffering injuries; in hating slothfulness; in always finding occupation, and being ever watchful. O brother, do you endeavor to practice diligently these precepts in order that your soul may not become a den of most vicious affections.

Labour at each one of them with alacrity, so as not to render void and unfruitful this brief course of your life"

—St. John Damascene (*Parall. Lib. iii. cap. 84*)

---

[45] Matt. 18.3.
[46] Matt. 22:39, Rom. 13:10.

8.

"THE true humility of the faithful soul lies in this: not to pride one's self upon anything; not to murmur against anyone; not to be ungrateful, nor complaining, nor querulous; but in all things to thank God and to praise Him, Whose works are either justice or mercy.

Hence, whatsoever may befall you, always return thanks to the Lord."

—St. Anselm (*Comm. in* 1 *Thess. cap.* 5)

9.

"*I am the flower of the field and the lily of the valley*".[47] "*The just shall spring as the lily.*"[48] Who else is just but the humble? Jesus, Lord as He was, bowed beneath the hands of His servant, the Baptist; and to the Baptist, standing awestricken at His majesty, He exclaimed: "*Suffer it to be so now, for so it becometh us to fulfil all justice:*"[49] thereby evidently showing, that He placed the fulfilment of all justice in humility. The just man, therefore, is a humble man, the just man is the *valley*. If we also be found humble, we likewise shall spring up as the lily, and we shall flower for all eternity before the Lord.

Will not Jesus, indeed, then show Himself to be more especially the lily of the valley, when "*He will reform the body of our lowness, made like to the body of His glory.*"[50] The Apostle does not say our body, but *the body of our lowness*, in order to point out that the humble will be illuminated by and clothed

---

47 Cant. 2:1.
48 Hos. 14:6.
49 Matt. 3.15.
50 Phil. 3:21.

in that wonderful and ever enduring candour of the lily. This is what was to be said on the protest made by the Spouse of the sacred Canticles, that He was the Flower of the field and Lily of the valley."

—St. Bernard (*Super Cantica Ser.* 47)

10.

"TRUE humility makes no display of being such, and does not speak much of itself, because it not only desires to hide all other virtues, but more especially seeks to conceal itself. Were it lawful to make use of falsehood, deceit, and bad example, it would perform acts of arrogance and haughtiness so as to remain concealed under these subterfuges, and there to live unknown and secure. Hearken, then, to my advice: either let us never speak at all about humility, or if we do, let what we express outwardly be prompted by a true interior feeling. Never let us cast down our eyes without also humbling our hearts. Let us not appear desirous of being among the lowest, unless we really wish it. The truly humble man prefers others to say of him that he is a wretch, that he is of no account, that he is a good-for-nothing, rather than say so of himself. At all events, when he hears others speaking ill of him, he will by no means contradict them, but agree with them readily, because believing it all true himself, he is glad also to see others share his opinion."

—St. Francis of Sales (*Phil. Par.* 7. *cap.* 5.)

11.

"WHEN you are offered an insult, bear it with patience, and increase your love towards him who shows you contempt.

This is the touchstone for ascertaining whether or not a man be humble and holy. If he yields to resentment, although he should work miracles, put him down as a tottering reed. Father Balthesar Alvarez used to say, that the time of humiliations was the time for heaping up treasures of merit. You will gain more by accepting an insult with patience, than by fasting ten days on bread and water. The humiliations which are self-imposed are good, but to accept the humiliations which we receive from others is far more profitable, because in these latter there is much less of self, and more of God. Hence, there is much greater merit if we know how to bear them patiently. But to what good can a Christian pretend if he cannot bear an insult for the sake of God? What contempt has Jesus Christ not suffered for us,—blows, derisions, scourgings, spittings in the face! Ah! if we had true love for Jesus Christ, not only would we not resent affronts, but even be delighted at finding ourselves despised as He Himself was despised.

—St. Alphonsus Liguori (*Oper. Spirit*)

12.

"OFTENTIMES it is very profitable for the keeping us in greater humility that others know and reprehend our faults. When a man humbles himself for his defects he then easily appeases others, and quickly satisfies those that are angry with him.

The humble man God protects and delivers; the humble man He loves and comforts; to the humble He inclines Himself; to the humble He gives grace, and after he has been depressed raises him to glory. To the humble He reveals His secrets, and sweetly draws and invites him to Himself. The humble man having received reproaches maintains himself well enough in peace, because he is fixed in God and not in the world.

Never think that you have made any progress till you look upon yourself as inferior to all."

> — Thomas à Kempis (*The Imitation of Christ. Lib. 2. cap. 2*)

13.

"IT is the common opinion of theologians that he who has a greater degree of charity will enjoy in a higher degree the light of heavenly glory. This glory will be given only to the humble of heart, because true charity stoops to lowly things that it may ascend to things that are lofty. But why do you grow proud in the midst of earthly pomp, O dust and ashes, you mass of rottenness and food of worms! If you would be abashed and ashamed of yourself, obtain a clear knowledge of yourself. The root of all evil is pride; that of all good is charity. But you will not be able to implant charity, until you have first pulled up pride by the roots. How to uproot it will be taught you by charity. Charity alone knows how to resist the spirit of pride. You will resist the spirit of pride if you hide your virtues, and lay bare your defects. Be, therefore, very watchful and pay special attention to this, that the vice of pride consists chiefly in your unwillingness to tolerate from others any reproach for those faults of which you are ever ready to accuse yourself."

> —Cardinal Bona (*De Art. Div. Am. cap. 19*)

14.

"*IF any man thinketh himself to be something, whereas he is nothing, he deceiveth himself.*"[51] Consider that if this saying, which the Apostle proposes for your meditation, were well understood, it would put an end to all vain glory. How is it that so many get prouder from day to day? "*The pride of them that hate thee ascendeth continually.*"[52] Because from day to day they become more blinded in the knowledge of themselves. They think within themselves, that of themselves they are something, whereas in truth they are absolutely nothing. Hearken, therefore, to that general declaration of the Apostle, which applies to all alike: *If anyone*, be he who he may, *thinketh himself to be something*, he does not say something great—no! but simply, *something—if anyone thinketh himself to be something, whereas he is nothing, he deceiveth himself.* This, therefore, is the sublime truth that ought at last to convince you, that of yourself *thou art nothing—Nihil es.* And why? Because you of yourself have nothing except sin, which is the supreme nothing. Everything that you have outside of sin is all of God. The deepening of one's knowledge of this truth is the way to arrive at true humility; for although the essence of humility consists in the lowly submission of the will, yet the standard by which the will fixes the degree of its greater or less self-abasement, comes only from the intellect.

—Father Paul Segneri (*Mann. dell An. 11. Agost*)

---

[51] Gal. 6:3.
[52] Ps. 73:23.

15.

"WHEN you are praised and honored by others, unite yourself to the contempts, the derisions, the insults suffered by the Son of God. Take it for granted that a soul truly humble finds as much humiliation in honors, as it does in the midst of contempt. It acts like the bee, which gathers its honey no less from the dew that falls upon the absynth, as from that which drops upon the rose."

—St. Vincent of Paul

16.

"MY children, be humble: be lowly."

—St. Philip Neri.

Prayer

To implore the grace of devotion and of humility

"O Lord, my God, You are all my good, and who am I that I should dare speak to You? I am Your most poor servant and a wretched little worm, much poorer and more contemptible than I can conceive or dare express. Yet remember, O Lord, that I am nothing, I have nothing, and can do nothing. You alone are good, just, and holy: You can do all things, You give all things, You fill all things, leaving only the sinner empty. Remember Your tender mercies, and fill my heart with Your grace. You will not have Your works to be empty. How can I support myself in this wretched life, unless Your mercy and grace strengthen me? Turn not Your face from me, delay not Your visitation, withdraw not Your comfort, lest my soul become as earth without water to You. O Lord, teach me to do Your will, teach me to converse worthily and humbly in Your sight: for You are my wisdom, Who knows me in truth, and did know me before the world was made, and before I was born into the world."

—Thomas à Kempis (*The Imitation of Christ*, 3. *cap.* 3).

www.ingramcontent.com/pod-product-compliance
Lightning Source LLC
Chambersburg PA
CBHW070934120626
46546CB00004B/1411